BÔ YIN RÂ

THE BOOK
ON
SOLACE

For more information about the books
of Bô Yin Râ and titles published
in English translation, visit
The Kober Press web site at
www.kober.com.

BÔ YIN RÂ
(J. A. SCHNEIDERFRANKEN)

THE BOOK
ON
SOLACE

TRANSLATED BY
B.A. REICHENBACH

THE
KOBER
PRESS

BERKELEY, CALIFORNIA

For permission to quote or excerpt, write to:

THE KOBER PRESS
2534 Chilton Way
Berkeley, California 94704

or email: koberpress@mindspring.com

This book is a translation from the German of the second edition of *Das Buch des Trostes* by Bô Yin Râ, first published in 1924. The copyright to the German original is held by Kober Verlag AG, Bern, Switzerland.

Printed in the United States of America

Library of Congress Catalog Card Number: 96-076167

International Standard Book Number: 0-915034-05-0

Typesetting and design by Irene Imfeld, Berkeley, CA

Book cover after a design by Bô Yin Râ

TO THE MEMORY OF
MY MOTHER
EDITH REICHENBACH
1908–1993

CONTENTS

CHAPTER ONE

ON GRIEF AND
FINDING SOLACE

THERE SURELY are not many who have made their way across the heights and through the valleys of this earthly life of whom it might be said that they had never been in need of solace in their grief.

But, then, those few most likely wanted inner depth; for it is certainly no proof of special moral strength if one does not, at any time, feel need of comfort in one's sorrow.

∽

WHEN TEMPESTS have disturbed an ocean's calm, its surging tides need longer to subside than will the ripples of a shallow pond. So, too, a human soul of depth and substance tends to be profoundly stirred by all of life's ordeals—indeed, may suffer their effects long afterward—while shallow souls, who are not troubled very deeply, will overcome their anguish from one day to the next.

Thus, only souls whom grief and pain have shaken to their roots have truly need of solace; souls who are at risk of seeing their despair embitter every source of future joy in life.

There are more human souls in need of comfort on this earth than there are poor who need material help; and of that kind of poverty the world has certainly more than enough.

Regrettably, it only is in days of grief that many gain a fleeting sense of their potential depth; because in times of joy, whose influence could truly be no less profound, they will content themselves with superficial trifles.

❧

IT IS QUITE true that, in the light of higher insight, all suffering in mortal life reveals itself as falsehood, rooted in illusion. But even falsehood, in the end, must serve the victory of truth. So too, all grief, of which the earth engenders such excess, is ultimately destined to assure the triumph of abiding joy.

And herein finally resides the true strength of all solace; if solace would be more than simply persuasion, aimed at making you forget your grief.

But seeking to forget your pain will only let its spurious claims the more unfailingly deceive you.

If you intend to make your anguish serve the truth, you certainly shall not desire to forget it.

Instead, you need to learn courageously to face, and then to overcome the grief that has befallen you. To overcome, however, does not mean you should forget. And it would gain you even less if cowardly you turned to flight in order to escape your grief. In short, if you attempted to dispel one falsehood by succumbing to another.

❧

BE ASSURED, the world's great masters in the art of living have never timidly avoided pain and grief.

They had the strength to bear affliction, but equally could rise to the experience of great joy.

They recognized that every grief becomes a pledge, indeed, a precondition of ensuing joy—if but one's consciousness of pain is liberated from the spell of falsehood, of illusion.

❧

YOU SURELY cannot keep your life protected from all grief. You can, however, change the way you face its pain, and thus deflate its falsely granted moral "worth." And, truly, all the pain that you must bear in life is set before you only as a task— that you devalue its imagined "merits."

This approach alone will free you from your compulsive servitude to grief and cause you to become its conqueror and master.

Only thus shall you experience grief in such a way that it must benefit your inner growth, whereas before its pain had threatened to destroy you.

⁂

I⊤ ɪs, surely, not too difficult to deal with grief in mortal life if you regard it from that point of view. On the other hand, you never shall grow strong enough to overcome your pain if you lack courage to confront it.

Only those who have the strength to suffer grief in every fiber of their soul shall also, in the end, grow able to discern that all its pain in truth reflects a lie.

Then only will they know how to dispel their grief, and thus attain the highest kind of solace, whose light they shall see rising from the inmost certainty of having found the source of all-sustaining truth.

&

AND ONLY comfort of that kind is worthy of the name of solace, which is to be the topic of this book.

I here intend to show you how one may come to find such solace—within one's inmost self —and then shall have no further need to be consoled by others.

No consolation you receive from others can ever free you from the shackles of your grief—unless such comfort teaches you how you may break those chains yourself. And how that inner art is learned, and put to use, the present work will teach you.

CHAPTER TWO

LESSONS ONE CAN LEARN FROM GRIEF

YOUR FATE on earth may well have struck you cruel blows.

You feel abandoned to their vengeance, a helpless victim at the mercy of a power that forces you to suffer, owing to some hidden law that human understanding cannot grasp.

Tightly fettered by the bonds of ancient speculation, your mind in vain attempts to find a "sinful" deed, some "wrong" you have committed, as "punishment" for which you might explain the harm that has befallen you.

❧

WITH THIS IDEA, however, you entrap yourself already in a first insidious delusion;
for there is nowhere any such "avenger"
having power, as imagined by that blind
belief of ancient days, to mete out
"penance" for your "guilt."

❧

TO BE SURE, each action in itself contains
its inescapably determined consequence,
and no one ever shall be able to evade the
repercussions of his deeds. However, you
may also be afflicted by suffering and
grievous pain that certainly did not result
from anything you might have done.

Do not yourself make grief that you must
suffer even worse by harboring tormenting
thoughts, in the erroneous belief that, if
you could but trace the cause of your dis-
tress to something you have done, your
anguish might be lessened.

✤

Iᴇ sᴏᴍᴇ calamity has struck you, above all else do not allow it time to gain a foothold in your thoughts; for if it once has overwhelmed your mind you will not easily escape again from its possessive grip.

Rise up, assert yourself at once and seek a firm foundation in your inmost self, so that you may successfully confront and wrestle with the forces that are seeking to defeat you.

✤

Yᴏᴜ ᴍᴜsᴛ ʙᴇ master in your mind and soul, allowing nothing to defy your will, not even grief; no matter how profoundly you might feel its power.

Only in this frame of mind can you indeed encounter solace in yourself.

Solace is of value only as a counter-force: an energy that lends one strength to overcome the hostile force of grief.

❧

To BE SURE, if you would find the strength of lasting solace, you have to probe the ground that underlies your grief.

You then, however, shall discover that, at the very bottom of your grief, there is at work a busy lie that would persuade you to believe that now all light has been extinguished in your life, that every source of inner joy is henceforth doomed to perish in despair.

If you are willing to believe that lie, its power over you will grow to be almost invincible.

It then shall feed itself by preying on the lifeblood of your heart and, like a vampire you cannot see, it slowly will despoil you of your strength, of all your will to live.

Then, indeed, will everything that once had filled your life with radiant light be swallowed by the depth of gloomy night.

For that reason I advise you to be ever on your guard, and not to trust the lie inherent in all grief.

Resolutely turn your back on its allure, lest its power, like Medusa's eyes, confound and paralyze your will. Instead, consistently remind yourself by saying:

It is not true that every ray of light
has now forever been extinguished!

It is not true that I shall never see the
sun display its power in my life again!

It is not true that earthly grief could
ever triumph over timeless joy!

❧

BUT MOST of all, remember always that this very pain, which would appear to you all but unbearable, can only hold you in its grip because you do not yet discern the truth that is kept hidden at the bottom of all grief by the persuasive power of that lie.

The more decisively you will reject that lie's disdainful sneer, the sooner will the truth, which is obscured behind your grief, appear to you in its majestic glory.

Those who have perceived that truth gain strength to master even the most bitter pain; for now they are aware that grief in all its forms must needs disintegrate and vanish when its time has come.

∞

No GRIEF is everlasting, and you alone have power to prolong its life beyond its given span.

Still, in a mysterious way, all grief contains the promise of a joy to come. Notwithstanding that today you might resent it as quite heartless mockery if one attempted in this way to make you see the anguish that you suffer in the light of final truth.

The lie inherent in all grief still has a rigid hold on you and it seduces you to nurse, indeed to love, the pain you suffer. And thus you feel offended if one would speak to you of joy, whose very essence is eternal; just as grief is, by its nature, bound to end in time.

Your mind still trembles from the anguish of your senses, nor is your will yet master of your raging thoughts.

And so you constantly rekindle memories, reminding you of things that used to be, before you had been struck by grief. But in this way you keep yourself from recognizing your present new reality, while that which you have lost grows ever larger in your mind.

❧

NONETHELESS, your grief—however agonizing it might be—can yet become a blessing in your life. On the other hand, it likewise may remain a cause of never ending harm, unless you find a way to force it to obey your will.

You alone decide what fruit your soul shall harvest from the seed which grief has planted in your life.

Only when you shall no longer look back to the past, but recognize that all your work from now on lies before you, shall you indeed reap blessings from your pain.

⌁

YOUR LIFE presents you with a challenge whenever it conducts your way through suffering and grief.

Every such experience is both an ending and the start of something new.

If you abide too long with what has ended, you greatly weaken your most precious energies, which ought to help you forge a new beginning.

I SURELY AM not one who has an interest in keeping you subservient to the fiction that all the suffering on earth is sanctioned by "God's will"; nor that it always is determined, even in its most abhorrent forms, by inescapable necessity.

On the contrary, I can reliably assure you that by far the greatest part of all the misery on earth would have an end, if human minds were not in fact so ready to expect it.

This alone, however, will prevent the earth from ever being wholly free of suffering.

You should not live in constant expectation of impending harm, nor willfully attract it by your hidden fears. But when some ill has struck you, always bear in mind that your own life in some way seeks to guide you to a higher path.

Do not impede your own advance by looking only downward into the abyss, but raise your sights above yourself and thus attempt to recognize what claims your life still has on you, rather than yourself at all times making claims upon your life. Claims that, for the most part, may seem "valid" only from the limited horizon of your purely physical perspective.

The recognition of the claims your life still has on you when it compels you to encounter grief will offer you that strength of solace which you would seek in vain as long as you keep looking only to the past.

CHAPTER THREE

ON FOLLIES
TO AVOID

IF YOU WOULD find enduring solace in yourself you must not blindly delve into your grief, nor constantly reopen wounds that are about to heal.

⚭

RESOLUTELY SHOW the door to all who come ostensibly to "comfort" you, but know of nothing better than digging up new graves.

The grief you have experienced needs peace and quiet in your soul, that it may come to rest within your depth.

Only when it is embedded in your inner-most—as a possession you can never lose—will it become a source to fill you with new life.

⁂

ALL GRIEF is only powerful as long as you embrace it, and willingly endure its yoke.

But if you, after having faced and suffered grief, no longer grant it power to oppress you, its might is at an end.

Therefore, grief is ever anxious to remind you of its presence and its claims.

Like all things that are granted but a brief existence, grief too desires to prolong its life, and to enjoy its powers, beyond its given term.

To that effect, however, you need to lend it your support; for without you it has no way to stay alive.

Now to endear itself to you as something truly precious, it cunningly will always choose the most seductive masks.

❧

How THOROUGHLY, through all of human history, has it beclouded mortal minds in order to be seen as a divinely chosen messenger, indeed as proof of "God's" concern and love!

Human minds thus even learned to love their grief, without suspecting that, according to inherent laws which govern this external world, such love must of necessity increase the suffering on earth.

❧

AMONG THIS PLANET'S elemental forces, there are, however, unseen physical intelligences which have no greater interest than seeing human beings suffer, because these hidden leeches nourish and renew themselves through human energies, and human souls at no time prove a better and more willing prey than when they suffer grief.

The more a person's suffering can be intensified—raised from a feeling that is still controlled, into a blind, tyrannical obsession—the easier it is for those elusive predators to rob their victims of the energies they crave.

And thus they will resort to every means within their power in order to protract a person's grieving to the utmost limit.

It is no accident that people who have suffered long and bitter grief appear as if they had been drained of energy and strength.

Indeed, their inner vigor has been drawn from them by every ruse and ploy, while all the time they nearly reveled in their grief, calling it the nicest names—indeed, promoting it to "holy" rank—in order to feel justified completely to immerse themselves in pain.

And in this way will human beings let their souls become a willing prey for the vampiric predators and werewolves that have their place in the invisible dimension of this planet.

If such abuse is ever to be curbed, one needs to be aware of these realities, and thus to strip all suffering of its unconscious pleasure. And, truly, there is more perverted pleasure in all grief than those who suffer ever would suspect.

It is true that people do not covet grief as a potential source of pleasure.

Again, there surely is no pleasure in enduring pain whose force a person still is able to control.

Nonetheless, as soon as grief has overwhelmed a person's will, so that he now desires to embrace his pain, his instinct finds a morbid satisfaction in constantly reopening his wounds. To be sure, the person neither realizes what occurs, nor would be willing to admit it. Yet in this way the loathsome, unseen parasites which feed on such a victim's blood can satisfy their craving.

It is these creatures that one must escape. And even though this earth shall never be completely free of suffering, one can in fact restrict it to its very limits, which are determined by necessity as a result of laws that govern physical reality.

All grief that lies beyond the limits which these laws impose, whatever is not justified by physical causality, can in time be purged from human life on earth. And this is done already in the life of every individual who realizes on his own that human beings merely sacrifice themselves to their invisible tormentors if they succumb to the delusion which, since ancient times, has sanctioned human grief as something all but holy.

To be sure, one should not misinterpret what I here explain.

I truly feel profound respect for all who suffer grief, yet seek to bear their pain with dignity the while it has to be endured; for all who then surmount their grief, and thus secure within themselves the deepest source of solace, whose comfort guides them to a new and heightened life; the kind of comfort no external solace can provide.

I only warn against abandoning oneself to grief and, thus, against the superstition of treating human suffering as something "holy" and decreed by "God." For in reality, all grief is rooted in a lie and evil. Even where it must be borne in consequence of inescapable necessity, it only manifests the imperfection of this physical domain of life.

⁓

I THUS REGARD it as a patent blasphemy if one feels no compunction to equate a "God"—who is proclaimed as being Love—with the lemurian parasites which, in this planet's occult twilight realm, engorge themselves with energies of human life. Yet this unwitting sacrilege is propagated by the teaching: "Whom God loves, He disciplines."

Had this notion not been fathered by the folly of a sage, one would have to denounce it as a crime against humanity.

In its effects, however, it proved certainly no less. And cunningly have the demonic predators, who once had planted this delusion in a human mind, succeeded in assuring that the folly which had long ago embraced that thought would then continuously generate still further pain.

⁂

IF ONE WOULD not be guilty of the misery this concept has already caused, and may continue to produce in future, since it instructs the human mind to love and nourish what in truth is evil, then let each person bear the grief allotted him in life with courage, dignity, and sober recognition of its bitterness—until it has been overcome. But one must not presume to raise one's grief as such to the exalted rank of a divinely sanctioned favor, just because the way a person bears his pain can purify his inner life.

What human beings have to suffer is not some "fate" directed from "on high," but rather, in each instance, the inevitable consequence of factors and events at work within the realm of physical perception. Unless that suffering has been unknowingly attracted and increased by virtue of a person's faith in its alleged "sanctity," and the belief in its divine intent.

⚮

Whether at this time you are oppressed by grief, or feel your spirit free of sorrow, never fail to tell yourself each day anew:

All suffering is but an evil that I must surmount.

All suffering is evil, and I beseech the Spirit to be spared its pain as far as laws of nature will allow.

All suffering is evil, and I shall not contribute to its increase here on earth; be it through my fear, by which it is attracted, nor by my faith in its alleged "sanctifying" grace.

ALL EXPERIENCE in this present life can serve you as a test to prove your inner worth, and likewise can your grief. But you will hardly find that someone failed to prove himself at other times, yet suddenly revealed great stature in his grief.

If your impression would seem otherwise, you well may have misjudged the way that person lived his life.

You must, of course, not overlook the fact that all of life's experiences can greatly further inner growth; and I do not mean to imply that someone might not benefit from having to experience grief. It is not grief as such, however, that may prove beneficial to a person's growth, but rather his approach to all of life's experiences. And it is that approach which manifests his real worth, also during times of pain.

To be sure, the highly rated school of sorrow and contrition may well have broken many self-assured and haughty minds, so that they meekly crept back to the Cross. One ought not to deceive oneself, however, but rather first examine whether such a discipline had truly raised the person to the peak of his potential, or only so profoundly crushed, demoralized, and wearied him that he no longer had the strength courageously to lift his head.

Listless resignation may often look like extraordinary kindness, while in fact it only shows a human will destroyed by grief; an apathy devoid of every wish and drive; a state of mind in which a person's inability to conquer sorrow has robbed this present life of every value worth possessing.

⚭

You MAY REGARD all those with skepticism who were supposedly made "better" human beings by virtue only of their having suffered grief.

Either they had all along been better than you thought; were able to discern what was demanded of them by their life; and thus had risen to surmount their grief to seek a new beginning—or what you see are merely broken wills, whose listless gestures of indifference appear like deep compassion.

❧

Souls who probe the very depth of grief, but afterwards rise up to overcome their sorrow; souls who lift their eyes to goals that lie ahead, and bravely set out to begin anew, may often seem the least affected by their pain. Yet they above all others reap the greatest blessings from their grief.

For it is such who found the strength of solace in their own eternal self and then were able to reveal that comfort: in themselves and through their conduct in this life.

Yet hardly will they be so foolish as to look upon the pain they had to suffer as if it were a special sign of love from heaven.

CHAPTER FOUR

ON THE
COMFORTING
VIRTUE OF WORK

No PERSON, truly, could be poorer and more wretched—and if he owned the wealth of all the world—than one who does not realize the infinite potential for strengthening all his capacities, which he possesses in the gift for work.

⚬

Now IN THIS life there are all kinds of work that need to be performed, and many people might assume that only if it serves a lofty purpose could their work prove beneficial to their highest inner senses.

But those who hold that view still do not know the real blessings that reside in work, and thus would likely misinterpret what I seek to tell them.

❧

THAT IS TO SAY, what I discuss is not the fact that certain types of work might give you special pleasure; although I truly hope you find your daily work enjoyable.

Again, I do not question that working for a cause which you regard as of the highest worth can prove an inspiration for your mind and soul.

Besides, there is an underlying misconception in respect to work that should be dealt with at the outset.

❧

PERHAPS YOU KNOW of someone who is able to devote himself to a creative, lofty task, while you, by contrast, have to toil for daily wages, performing merely common chores, be it with your hands or with your mind.

Quite possibly you feel a touch of secret envy, because your lot on earth, your talents, or your schooling have denied you access to an occupation you consider equally creative and fulfilling.

Yet, in reality, you have no cause at all to harbor envy toward another.

❧

BECAUSE—no matter what your occupation in this life might be—you indirectly are participating in that other person's work.

❧

THE LONGSHOREMAN unloading cargo in the harbor has just as much a share in every great achievement that his nation has attained through any of its members as does the worker whose machine converts those goods from distant lands into commercial products for consumption.

The peasant who is ploughing his field, the bookkeeper writing at his desk—all alike participate in the endeavors of the "other," in whose searching mind already lies prepared the medical discovery that is to bring a cure for some disease; or of another, who labors night and day in order that the fruits of his research might benefit the world, today and in the future.

⸙

AGAIN, THOSE "others" would indeed be foolish to believe that all of their accomplishments were owing to themselves alone.

To be sure, as poets, artists, or as specialists in their respective fields they are the authors of their own creations. Yet those creations in themselves would never see the light of day except for the far-reaching network of essential contributions made by other hands and minds. For only through the labor of innumerable others are conditions brought about that will allow creative talents to pursue their work.

⚬

I ONE DAY heard about a little group of kindred spirits who were convinced that they could lead the perfect life if they were ready to get rid of all the things they had not wrought with their own hands.

As a result, those sensitive idealists proceeded to "return to nature" and settled down in solitary wilderness.

The only thing they would not be without was—books. And another—a splendid concert grand, on which a highly gifted member of the group would play the works of great composers.

And in this way they plainly demonstrated, by their very actions, the true absurdity of their utopian gospel. Ironically, however, they themselves remained oblivious to that fact.

One only has to think a minute to realize how many hands and special skills are needed merely to produce the raw material for a single book! Let alone, how many workers and machines have to collaborate to build a concert grand of perfect sound!

❧

I ONLY MENTION this experience here in passing because it shows so very clearly how all the greatest values that a culture can create and offer to the world entirely depend upon the ordinary working skills of countless heads and hands.

❧

No MATTER how prosaic a person's occupation may appear to his own mind, he nonetheless may be quite certain that, in one way or another, his labor indirectly has its share in even the sublimest works of his contemporaries. And on the other hand, the works of those creative spirits, although they might seem far removed from daily cares and worries, provide the only firm assurance that a society is able to sus-

tain its culture, and can provide well-pay-
ing work to even the most humble of its
members.

⚬

THAT ERROR, and its consequences, having
been set right, let us consider now the
greatly heightened energy that one is able
to attain within one's soul by virtue of performing work—of any kind—provided
only it is done with single-minded concentration. It is the energy thus gained,
however, which also most effectively will
strengthen the power of true solace during
times of grief.

⚬

YOU DOUBTLESS know already from experience that even the distressing need of having to take care of matters that your grief
is likely to entail deflects your mind from
self-tormenting thoughts, allowing you to
find yourself, and thus to contemplate

what has befallen you in a more peaceful state of mind.

Now if you are to find the strongest solace in your soul, it is above all else essential that your thoughts shall not continuously dwell upon and cleave to what you suffer.

The easiest and best way to prevent this is by concentrating so completely on a given task that, while you are performing it, no other thoughts can occupy your mind.

In times of grief, the hours that you spend at work—provided you are working as one ought to work—will always be a respite that allows you to recover from tormenting thoughts.

⁂

This advice, however, is not meant for those who only *think* they "work," be it with their hands or with their mind, while in effect their roaming thoughts routinely tend to be on other things. Yet I doubt that any such have real need of solace; except it be the kind that will, in their accustomed fashion, allow them to forget their grief.

I here address myself to souls who suffer grief in all its depth, and who are ready to employ their will in order to surmount it.

⸎

Nothing will more surely bring you solace of the kind that manifests itself in you as strength, which teaches you to deal with even the most bitter grief, than shall your daily work—performed the way all work must be performed if its effect should benefit your soul.

No other path shall more directly guide you to a new beginning.

⸎

Seeing that you are a person searching for the Spirit's life, I must expect that you will not approach whatever work you do, no matter how "mechanical" it seems, so casually that it will let you, at the same time, think of matters not directly bearing on your task. In the manner of convivial grannies in a knitting circle, who do not ply their skill as work, but rather as a playful occupation for their fingers, which calls for their attention only now and then.

In fact, I must expect that you, a person who is willing to pursue the path that leads one to the Spirit, shall brook no interruption of your work, unless fatigue obliges you to rest.

⚭

ONLY BY performing work with total concentration will you experience the support that you require on your inner path. Besides, it will allow you to become the best among your fellow workers. And when you suffer grief, it is again such work that lets you find the healing strength of solace in yourself.

Those alone who know of working in that manner have truly earned their rest when they are done. Yet even their repose shall not be lacking in rewards; for they will then participate—by way of mental influences, according to their inner faculties—in benefits provided them through other people's work.

And when in times of grief you seek the healing strength of solace by thus performing all your work, you further shall receive profoundest inner comfort when, afterwards, you are at rest. Such comfort has its source within the Spirit's world, but only in a state of balanced inner calm, which you restored within yourself through concentrated work, shall you be able to receive it.

I HAVE MYSELF known work and grief from childhood on, and thus can speak to you as someone who has thoroughly experienced both.

You could put trust in my advice, even if I had no right besides to offer inner guidance.

Already as a child my life acquainted me with suffering of many kinds, and also later guided me along the various paths I had to make my own, so that today I would be competent to help wherever help can be extended through instruction.

⚘

In the aftermath of the Great War and all its horrors, the world today still suffers from an all-pervasive weariness. Nor is it understood as yet that only work, constructively performed for its own sake, will finally succeed in overcoming even this condition.*

Also here one can attain effective inner solace only through the wondrously regen-

* The first edition of this work appeared in 1924.— Translator's note.

erative force of work that is performed with perfect concentration.

⁂

I SURELY do not mean to ask you to "believe" in what I say.

Let those who suffer grief, or have grown weary of their toil and worries, put these counsels to the test!

It will not take them long to find out whether there is truth in what I say.

From work they shall derive the strength of inner solace—and sooner than they might expect. That very strength will free them from their burden and lend them energy to make a new beginning.

CHAPTER FIVE

ON SOLACE IN BEREAVEMENT

L IFT YOUR EYES, let not despair dishearten you in grieving for a soul you loved in life, and treasure still, but whom you had to bury.

Do not lose courage, mother, who has lost a child; you, father, from whose side a son was torn when he already had become a friend. Nor you, that had to see a parent's casket taken to its grave.

❧

I N TRUTH, you now may count it as a blessing if the religious teachings you received in youth were able to inform you with so deep a faith that it is able to sustain you even in this hour.

Thus, you were told the human soul would enter everlasting glory in the sight of God, and even this material body would one day celebrate its resurrection.

If this is truly your belief, why does your anguish seem so inconsolable?

I deeply share your feelings and fully understand what you have lost the while you live on earth.

You certainly have cause to grieve, and I am conscious of your pain.

Still, do not the teachings of your faith proclaim that Death has lost his sting?

After all, the separation you lament is only brief. And if your life indeed is anchored in your faith, the thought alone that the departed whom you love is now alive among the blessed, forever free of all the anguish of this present life, should make your very heart exult with joy!

❧

Blest you are, indeed, if you wholeheartedly believe these teachings, so that nothing ever could dispirit you to doubt your faith.

❧

Allow your grief to have its due, and shed the tears you must for the beloved, whom you will not, in this your present life, be able to embrace again, nor see, nor hear.

The tears you weep are justified—for it is you that must remain behind. And in this present life you shall not ever find again what you still love.

❧

But, come the day when you yourself shall leave this mortal life, you shall be reunited —as your faith assures you—with those you once had lost on earth for but a little while, and then your joy shall know no end.

Fortunate you are, indeed, if this is what you still believe.

Your tears shall soon have dried, and in your faith you will experience all the solace that you need.

⚜

STILL, I KNEW of many who claimed to be of that belief, but nonetheless were utterly despondent in their grief.

In fact, I did know many who had such teachings on their lips, while in their hearts they felt their faith was mere pretense. Still, they continued to profess that creed, because it was the custom that one should publicly embrace it.

By far the greatest number that I met, however, had long ago abandoned all pretending, because in their opinion all such belief was nothing more than pious myth.

It was among such disenchanted souls that I had met the greatest number having need of inner solace and who, indeed, proved capable of finding it if they were shown the proper way.

❧

ONE DAY I REPROACHFULLY was asked by such a reader saying, "Why, then, are we taught these things, which in effect contain the truth, the way one narrates fairy tales, so that their worth is lost to us once we have reached the age when we no longer can believe in myths?"

Him I was obliged to leave with this advice, "Do not find fault with those who simply taught you what they knew, as best they could, but see to it, instead, that you yourself find better things to offer."

❧

THE SOLACE furnished by the ancient doctrines truly rests on solid ground and those who still are able to believe their teachings shall certainly not be deluded in the end. Even though the concepts molded from those doctrines do not entirely agree with spiritual reality.

They, nonetheless, will let one's mind intuitively sense the truth, by showing that the mortal body of this world was but the temporal, material means of self-expression of a being whose origin is not found on this earth. A being that, in every way, is manifest to mortal human senses only while it can reveal itself in the material form that is provided by this physical domain.

It surely is naive to foster the belief that one day there shall come to life another body, one consisting of the same material elements that mortal human senses can perceive. Yet even this belief contains in fact a truth; namely, that a human being's timeless spiritual form essentially reflects the person's former physical appearance; given that, in mortal life as well, it was the spiritual image that, more or less successfully, imprinted its own features on the human mortal form.

❧

It is also true that those whom death has separated in this present life shall one day "meet again" in life beyond. And at that time they will be able, in their spiritual forms, to recognize each other far more easily than, for instance, people here on earth who had not seen each other for some years.

❧

Entirely mistaken, on the other hand, is the assumption that no sooner has the human being's spiritual essence left its mortal organism than it will find itself surrounded by the "joys of heaven," or could fall prey to a condition of eternal agony from which it cannot ever find release.

❧

This latter concept, nonetheless, contains an element of truth; given that completely brutish, instinct-driven natures, who are excessively attached to mortal life, may well remain for aeons in a state of spiritual darkness before their souls grow able once again to apprehend the radiant substance of the Spirit's light.

Yet even here the Spirit's law, whose very life proceeds from love, is far more merciful than the vindictiveness of human judgment. And none who is remembered still with love on earth can ever find his soul the victim of such agonizing night for aeons, no matter how profoundly flawed his mortal life might once have been.

⚮

IN THE BOOK ON LIFE BEYOND* I have described in some detail the state in which the spiritual essence of a human being finds itself when its material body has turned cold. In that, and many of my other books, I also spoke about the source to which I owe the certainty that is required to discuss these matters.

*The Kober Press, 1978

May it suffice if here I only state that such objective certainty derives from thoroughly reliable experience. Saying this, I know full well that many readers in the Western cultures of our time must think it foolish and presumptuous if told that there, indeed, are human beings living on this earth who do possess the needed faculties to know such things from personal experience; even though such individuals are of necessity extremely rare.

❧

As to the state of consciousness, however, in which a person who has left this present life will reawaken on the other side, it should be known that this awakening initially occurs within a lower sphere of spiritual life; a sphere that still is very close to mortal life on earth.

If during mortal life the individual already had prepared itself for spiritual reality, it soon will leave this lower realm behind, safely guided on its way by helpers one can trust. Some of these guides may once themselves have lived on earth, like the departed, while others never knew existence in material form.

In the course of its ascent—the times required are no longer measurable in material terms—the human spirit then encounters also helpers who, still alive in mortal bodies, continue to be spiritually active here on earth, but at the same time function in that higher sphere of Spirit, where they are manifest in their immortal forms. These helpers, too, will guide the human spirit higher, to ever clearer knowledge and perception of eternal life.

This is the way that lies before all those who in their days on earth have taught themselves, by virtue of a life of action and of love, to recognize, in their essential nature, realities that were unknown to them before, and thus will consequently also follow the advice of those who here alone are competent to offer guidance in the life to come.

❧

THE MAJORITY, however, of the multitudes that leave this mortal life at any time are not at all unhappy in this lower border realm of spiritual existence once they realize that they are conscious, occupy a body, and can express their will through action. And so they now set out to find in this domain whatever might resemble the beliefs and notions they had held on earth.

Since in this realm, much like in dreams, all images conceived appear as tangible reality, the unprepared are mesmerized by their self-generated phantom world, and in this state will pay no more attention to the voice of those who could direct them to a higher plane than someone who is dreaming will necessarily awaken, despite the sound of voices that are heard nearby.

❧

A<small>ND</small> <small>GIVEN</small> that the mind of even those arriving with a guilty conscience will always know some grounds by which to justify themselves in their own eyes, they promptly rid their consciousness of all ideas that might at first have frightened them, such as the prospect of eternal "punishment," or agonies of purifying flames. Instead, they now perceive a realm of "heaven" wherein they find all things exactly as they had imagined and believed on earth.

Those, on the other hand, who thought their life would simply end together with their mortal organism, now will in the same way mold themselves a semblance of their former physical existence. And all who thus contribute to their envisioned phantom worlds are happy in a fashion, each in his own way. Until the day when finally their sleeping soul shall gradually awaken and come to recognize that the collectively engendered dream world of fulfillment had been no more than a mirage. Not unlike in mortal life a person roused from sleep will waken from his private, individual dreams.

Only after having thus awakened is the human spirit capable of hearing the protective helper's voice and then can grasp his offered hand. And now that spirit will begin to make its way, ascending to the Spirit's higher worlds: consciously developing its given faculties; patiently progressing step by step, ever closer to the worlds of radiant spiritual substance; gaining strength through manifesting love, and thus in turn attracted by the timeless source from which all Love proceeds.

❧

YET IN CASES when a human spirit that sought physical embodiment had found such self-expression in the body only of a child, and if that child had lived at least sufficient time to let its spiritual scintilla become united with the given elements that form its timeless soul, then such a spirit will indeed be conscious of its own existence, but has not yet acquired the faculty to mold itself a world of images and concepts drawn from memories of earthly life. Or, if that faculty already should exist, it then is still so undeveloped that its owner nonetheless is spared succumbing to the lure of some collective dream of bliss, in which adults may well entrap themselves for ages.

A spirit of that kind will then at once be taken by the hand and guided to a higher level by the helpers in the Spirit's world. And while it shall need far more time to climb the steps on its ascent, because it lacks the inner knowledge and experience it could have gained on earth, it does enjoy the benefit of being conscious, from the outset, in the light of truth and under the protection of unerring guides.

❧

As for being reunited and recognizing one another in the Spirit's world, such encounters only can take place if either the departed spirits had never entered the deceptive sphere of dreamlike wish fulfillment—save as a country hastily to be traversed—or after they have finally awakened from the phantom-bliss of such delusions, and then began their journey to the Spirit's higher worlds, knowingly directed by their inner guide.

From that time forth, however, such "reunions" can occur at any time. And that is true not merely of all those who personally had met each other here on earth, but also any that had simply known of one another; provided only that the bond between them had been one of inner sympathy. On the other hand, the different levels of their spiritual development do not preclude such contact.

A child torn from its mother's arms in early life will first appear to her exactly in the form that she had known on earth. Then, however, will her child transform itself, before her eyes, into its timeless nature in the Spirit.

☙

THUS, EVERYONE shall first behold the other
in a form reflecting the remembered like-
ness here on earth, only to perceive that
spirit afterwards in its eternally enduring
form. All this is possible, however, because the substance that embodies spiritual consciousness is able to assume the
shape of any image the human spirit's
consciousness may have of its own being.
And so, to give but one example, a person
born with some deformity, will first appear
"deformed" to those he meets again in life
beyond, since in their memory he only
does exist in this defective image. Yet
then he quickly will dispense with that
appearance, which now he clearly wants
to see ignored, in order to reveal himself,
unchanged in his identity, but in the full
perfection of his timeless form.

☙

ALTHOUGH THE things I here describe may sound more like ideas derived from fairy tales, they nonetheless reflect reality as accurately as if I were depicting physical events with which you are familiar, so that you easily could recognize them from experience.

Perhaps you rather ought to ask yourself whether certain concepts that have found expression in mythology might not in fact guide one's attention higher, to the human spirit's timeless home; even where the authors of such stories only sensed the truth unconsciously, through intuition.

⸎

AS YOU CAN SEE, however, even people like yourself, who are no longer able to believe what they were taught have access to the same, indeed, to far more solid grounds of comfort than are known to those who still find their contentment in their childhood's faith.

You may believe me when I say that I profoundly understand the pain you suffer, now that someone whom you loved is gone from you, and you no longer can enjoy that person's presence in this world of physical perception.

Beyond the burden of that pain, however, there truly is no cause for you to grieve. Notwithstanding that the physically departed, who now experience life through other means, are clearly not yet able to find themselves awake and active in the Spirit's highest realms, but even in their present state must first develop and perfect themselves; exactly as a person here on earth is bound to do, if he would spiritually accomplish that which can be realized in mortal life. To describe what that entails, however, is the aim of all my books.

⚭

ALSO BEAR in mind that, on the spiritual plane, you are by no means separated from the souls you loved who now have laid aside their mortal forms.

Within your inmost self—where you yourself are spirit—you and they remain connected by an inner bond. And should you want to learn and listen to your innermost, you will become increasingly more certain that you continue to be linked with them in spiritual ways.

⚬

Beware of all attempts, however, to summon the departed back into the realm of matter, hoping to perceive them with your mortal senses.

You cannot ever call the soul of a departed back to earth!

They now are far beyond the range of your five senses; nor could you ever reach them even if you mastered all the foolish spells and incantations collected through the ages by deluded necromancers.

❧

The only forces you might summon are creatures that would seek to fool you with a ghoulish farce. Besides, they would cause serious harm to both your body's and your soul's most precious energies.

❧

ON THIS SUBJECT, too, you will find some more detailed explanations elsewhere in my writings. Here I must refer you to those books, if I would not repeat what has been stated there.

❧

How YOU can find true solace in yourself, the present book has told you.

You now should put your grief behind you, and weep no longer for the souls who have passed on to their eternal home.

They henceforth have their own way to pursue, just as you must now continue to go yours.

Raise yourself and set out to begin anew. And if you thus resolve to find the way into the Spirit, then you shall likewise, even here on earth, receive the Spirit's help through unseen guides. The selfsame help that now is guiding also your departed loved ones to the light which is the human soul's eternal home.

❧

ABOVE ALL other things, however, let your life at all times be inspired by the will toward selfless love!

For none but souls imbued with love find guidance—be it here or in the life beyond—and not until the phantom realm of selfish dreams shall lie behind you will you yourself encounter highest love: the infinite, sublimest wellspring of all solace.

REMINDER

"YET HERE I must point out again that if one would derive the fullest benefit from studying the books I wrote to show the way into the Spirit, one has to read them in the original; even if that should require learning German.

"Translations can at best provide assistance in making readers gradually perceive, even through the spirit of a different language, what I convey with the resources of my mother tongue."

From Gleanings, "Answers to Everyone" (1933).
Bern: Kobersche Verlagsbuchhandlung, 1990.

By the same author:

The Book on the Living God

Contents: Word of Guidance. "The Tabernacle of God is with Men." The "Mahatmas" of Theosophy. Meta-Physical Experiences. The Inner Journey. The En-Sof. On Seeking God. On Leading an Active Life. On "Holy Men" and "Sinners." The Hidden Side of Nature. The Secret Temple. Karma. War and Peace. The Unity among Religions. The Will to Find Eternal Light. Mankind's Higher Faculties of Knowing. On Death. On the Spirit's Radiant Substance. The Path toward Perfection. On Everlasting Life. The Spirit's Light Dwells in the East. Faith, Talismans, and Images of God. The Inner Force in Words. A Call from Himavat. Giving Thanks. Epilogue.

The Kober Press, 1991. 333 pages, paperback. ISBN 0-915034-03-4

This work is the central volume of the author's *Enclosed Garden*, a cycle of thirty-two books that let the reader gain a clear conception of the structure, laws, and nature of eternal life, and its reflections here on earth. The present work sheds light on the profound distinction between the various ideas and images of "God" that human faith has molded through the ages—as objects for external worship—and the eternal spiritual reality, which human souls are able to experience, even in this present life. How readers may attain this highest of all earthly goals; what they must do, and what avoid; and how their mortal life can be transformed into an integrated part of their eternal being, are topics fully treated in these pages.

What sets this author's works on spiritual life apart from other writings on the subject is their objective clarity, which rests upon direct perception of eternal life and its effects on human life on earth. Such perception is only possible, as he points out, if the observer's spiritual senses are as thoroughly developed to perceive realities of timeless life, as earthly senses need to be in order to experience physical existence. Given that authentic insights gathered in this way have always been extremely rare, they rank among the most important writings of their time, conveying knowledge of enduring worth that otherwise would not become accessible.

The Book on Life Beyond

Contents: Introduction. The Art of Dying. The Temple of Eternity and the World of Spirit. The Only Absolute Reality. What Should One Do?

The Kober Press, 1978. 115 pages, paperback. ISBN 0-915034-02-6.

This book explains why life "beyond" is not so much a different and wholly other life, but rather the continuation of the self-same life we live on earth. The difference between the two dimensions lies chiefly in the organs of perception through which the same reality of life is individually experienced. On earth we know that life through our mortal senses, in life beyond it is perceived through spiritual faculties, which typically awaken after death. At that transition, the human consciousness, which usually is unprepared for the event, is at a loss and finds itself confused by the beliefs and concepts of its former mortal life. As a result, the new arrival faces certain dangers; for, owing to these mental prejudices, the person is unable to distinguish between perceptions of objective truth and the alluring phantom "heavens" generated by misguided faith on earth.

To help perceptive readers form correct and realistic expectations, that they may one day reach the other shore with confidence and without fear, this book provides trustworthy guidance into spiritual life, its all-pervading structure, laws, and inner nature. Given the unbreakable connection between our actions here on earth and their effects on life beyond, the book advises how this present life may best prepare the reader for the life that is to come.

The Book on Human Nature

Contents: Introduction. The Mystery Enshrouding Male and Female. The Path of the Female. The Path of the Male. Marriage. Children. The Human Being of the Age to Come. Epilogue. A Final Word.

The Kober Press, 2000, 168 pages, paperback, ISBN 0-915034-07-7

Together with *The Book on the Living God* and *The Book on Life Beyond*, *The Book on Human Nature* forms a trilogy containing guidelines toward a new and more objective understanding of both physical and spiritual realities, and of the human being's origin and place within these two dimensions of creation.

The Book on Human Nature at the outset shows the need to draw a clear distinction between the timeless spiritual component present in each mortal human, and the material creature body in which the spiritual essence is embodied during mortal life. The former, indestructible and timeless, owing to its being born of spiritual substance, represents the truly human element in what is known as mortal man. The latter, physical, contingent, and subject to decay and death, is no more than the temporary instrument the spiritual being uses to express itself in physical existence. Given that the spiritual and animal components within human nature manifest inherently discordant aspects of reality, they typically contend for domination of the total individual. Experience shows that in this conflict the animal component with its ruthless drives and instincts clearly proves the stronger.

To help the reader gain a realistic understanding of the human being's spiritual and physical beginnings, by way of concepts more in keeping with humanity's advances in every discipline of natural science, the book explains, to the extent that metaphysical events can be conveyed through language, the timeless origin and source of every human's spiritual descent. It likewise shows that the material organism, now considered mankind's primal ancestor, existed long before it was to serve the spiritual individuation as its earthly tool. In this context the author points out that the traditional creation story, such as it has survived, is not simply an archaic myth, invented at a time that lacked the benefits of modern knowledge, but instead preserves, in lucid images and symbols, a truthful view of actual events. Events, however, that did not happen merely once, at the beginning of creation, but are a process that continues even now, and will recur until this planet can no longer nurture human life.

Even so, the principal intention of the present work, as well as of the author's other expositions of reality, is not so much to offer readers a new, reliable cosmology, but rather to encourage them to rediscover and awaken the spiritual nature in themselves, and thus to live their present and their future life as fully conscious, truly human beings.

The Book on Happiness

Contents: Prelude. Creating Happiness as Moral Duty. "I" and "You". Love. Wealth and Poverty. Money. Optimism. Conclusion.

The Kober Press, 1994. 127 pages, paperback. ISBN 0-915034-04-2.

Sages and philosophers in every age and culture have speculated on the nature, roots, and attributes of happiness, and many theories have sought to analyze this enigmatic subject. In modern times, psychology has joined the search for concrete answers with its own investigations, which frequently arrive at findings that support established views. Still, the real essence of true happiness remains an unsolved riddle.

In contrast to traditional approaches, associating happiness with physical events, the present book points to the spiritual source from which all human happiness derives, both in life on earth and in the life to come. Without awareness of this nonmaterial fundament, one's understanding of true happiness is bound to be deficient.

The author shows that real happiness is neither owing to blind chance, nor a capricious gift of luck, but rather the creation of determined human will. It is an inner state that must be fostered day by day; for real happiness, as it is here defined, is "the contentment that creative human will enjoys in its creation." How that state may be created and sustained, in every aspect of this life, the reader can discover in this book.

The Wisdom of St. John

Contents: Introduction. The Master's Image. The Luminary's Mortal Life. The Aftermath. The Missive. The Authentic Doctrine. The Paraclete. Conclusion.

The Kober Press, 1975. 92 pages, clothbound. ISBN 0-915034-01-8.

This exposition of the Fourth Gospel is not a scholarly analysis discussing the perplexing riddles of this ancient text. It is, instead, a nondogmatic reconstruction of the actual events recorded in that work, whose author wanted to present the truth about the Master's life and teachings; for the image propagated by the missionaries of the new religion often was in conflict with the facts. The present book restores the context of essential portions of the unknown author's secret missive, which the first redactors had corrupted, so that its contents would support the other gospels.

Written by a follower of John, the "beloved disciple," its purpose was to disavow the "miracles" the other records had ascribed to the admired teacher. His record also is unique in that it has preserved the substance of some letters by the Master's hand, addressed to that favorite pupil.

Those writings are reflected in the great discourses which set this gospel text apart and lend it its distinctive tone.

Given the historic impact of the man presented in this work, an accurate conception of his life and message will not only benefit believers of the faith established in his name, but also may explain to others what his death in fact accomplished for mankind.

The Meaning of this Life

Contents: A Call to the Lost. The Iniquity of the Fathers. The Highest Goal. The "Evil" Individual. Summons from the World of Light. The Benefits of Silence. Truth and Verities. Conclusion.

The Kober Press, 1998, paperback. ISBN 0-915034-06-9.

This book addresses the most common questions people tend to ask at times when circumstances in their daily lives awaken their awareness of the many unsolved riddles that surround the human being here on earth. To be sure, philosophy and teachings of religion have offered answers to such questions through the ages, but as these often draw on speculation, or require blind belief, they can no longer truly satisfy the searching mind of our time.

It is against this background that the present book will guide its readers to a firmer ground of understanding, resting on objective insights and experience. From this solid vantage, readers may survey their own existence and its purpose with assurance.

As this book explains, the key to comprehending the meaning of this present life is, first, the insight that this life is but the consequence of causes in the Spirit's world and, thus, has of itself no meaning other than that fact. And, secondly, the recognition that material life is ultimately meaningless if human beings fail to give it meaning: by virtue of pursuing goals whose blessings shall endure. The nature of the highest goal that mortals can pursue provides the substance also of the present book.

About My Books, Concerning My Name, and Other Texts

Contents: Frontispiece portrait of the author. Translator's Foreword. About My Books. Concerning My Name. In My Own Behalf. Important Difference. Résumé. Comments on the Cycle Hortus Conclusus and the Related Works. The Works of Bô Yin Râ. Brief Biography of Bô Yin Râ.

The Kober Press, 1977. 73 pages, paperback. ISBN 0-915034-00-X.

This book presents selections from the author's works that let the reader gain a clear conception, both of the spiritual background and perspective of his writings, and of their extraordinary range and depth. For readers seeking knowledgeable guidance through the labyrinth of speculations, dogmas, and beliefs concerning final things, his expositions will provide a source of comfort and enduring light.

And since, from the "perspective of eternity," human beings bear responsibility to practice spiritual discernment, lest they be deceived by falsehoods, readers here will find reliable criteria to clarify their own beliefs regarding mysteries that neither mental powers nor religious faith have ever fully answered.

By showing that objective knowledge of spiritual existence is not only possible, but that attaining such experience is finally the foremost task of human life, these books become essential guides for readers seeking inner certainty, which mere belief cannot create. In this respect it is the practical advice these books provide which is their most remarkable characteristic.

Spirit and Form

Contents: The Question. Outer World and Inner Life. At Home and at Work. Forming One's Joy. Forming One's Grief. The Art of Living Mortal Life.

The Kober Press, 2000.

The underlying lesson of this book is that all life in the domain of spiritual reality, from the highest to the lowest spheres, reveals itself as lucid order, form, and structure. Spirit, the all-sustaining radiant substance of creation, is in itself the final source and pattern of all perfect form throughout its infinite dimensions. Nothing, therefore, can exist within, or find admittance to, the Spirit's inner worlds that is devoid of the perfection, harmony, and structure necessarily prevailing in these spheres.

Given that this present life is meant to serve the human being as an effective preparation for regaining the experience of spiritual reality, this life must needs be lived in ways that are consistent with the principles that govern spiritual reality; in other words, ought to be lived according to the structure, laws, and inner forms of that reality. To show the reader how this present life receives enduring form, which then is able to survive this mortal state, the book sheds light on crucial aspects of this physical existence and advises how these may be formed to serve one's spiritual pursuits.

THE
KOBER
PRESS

.

www.ingramcontent.com/pod-product-compliance
Lightning Source LLC
Chambersburg PA
CBHW022157080426
42734CB00006B/470